CLIFFORD BROWN

CONTENTS

Foreword

In recent years, with proliferation of transcribed solos and the growing awareness of their value as teaching tools, it has become apparent to many jazz educators that simply memorizing a solo and playing it is not maximizing the potential of the technique as a learning experience. By the inclusion of in depth analysis, selected discography and bibliography, biographical data, a list of innovations, a genealogy, etc., as well as actual transcriptions of important solos, these books represent an attempt to place the study of recorded solos in a more meaningful context.

In many respects the jazz improvisor is a composer and as such might profit from being exposed to the same regimen and disciplines as a composer *per se*. One such discipline has to do with learning to write or play by imitating various models. Virtually every composer has gone through the stage of writing pieces in the style of Bach, Bartok, Stravinsky, Ellington and others. In imitating a particular composer the neophyte must learn and assimilate the harmonic, melodic, and rhythmic language of that composer. He must be able to project in a reasonably accurate fashion what that composer will do, given a particular set of musical options. This type of learning experience becomes doubly important when the composer under scrutiny is one of the giants who in one area or another is responsible for transforming the aesthetic. For instance, in any given period a handful of innovators is responsible for introducing new concepts into the music or simply reinterpreting or reshaping the extant language consistent with imperatives of that time.

It seems to this writer that the jazz player might profitably adapt an approach similar to that of the budding composer in learning his craft. With that end in mind this series of style studies has been designed to provide a modus operandi for studying, analyzing, imitating and assimilating the idiosyncratic and general facets of the styles of various jazz giants throughout the history of the music.

Although a model styles and analysis work sheet is provided, the reader may want to modify it or design another one which fits his or her specific needs. In any event, the aspiring jazz player is encouraged to completely dissect the improvisations as well as the tunes on which they are based. (This is absolutely mandatory in the case of bebop tunes whose patterns, melodic lines and harmonic structures comprise a substantial portion of the vocabulary of every contemporary jazz musician).

Relationship Of Chords To Scales

Major Family

Chord Type (I)	Scale Form
Major — 1 3 5 7 9	Major 1 2 3 4 5 6 7 8
Major (♯4) 1 3 5 7 9 ♯11	Lydian 1 2 3 ♯4 5 6 7 8
Major (♯4 ♯5) 1 3 ♯5 7 9 ♯11	Lydian Augmented 1 2 3 ♯4 ♯5 6 7 8
Major (♭6 ♯9) 1 3 5 7 9 11 13	Augmented 1 ♯2 3 5 ♭6 7 1
Major 1 3 5 7 9	diminished 1 ♭2 ♭3 ♮3 ♯4 5 6 ♭7 8
Major 1 3 5 7 9	Harmonic Major 1 2 3 4 5 ♭6 7 8
Major 1 3 5 7 9	blues 1 ♭3 ♮3 4 ♯4 5 ♭7 8
Major 1 3 5 7 9	minor pentatonic 1 ♭3 4 5 ♭7 8
Major 1 3 5 7 9	Major pentatonic 1 2 3 5 6 8
	Seventh scale (Major) 1 2 3 4 5 ♯5 6 7 8

minor Family

Chord Type	Scale Form
minor, tonic (I) Function	Dorian 1 2 ♭3 4 5 6 ♭7 8
	Natural minor 1 2 ♭3 4 5 ♭6 ♭7 8
	Phrygian 1 ♭2 ♭3 4 5 ♭6 ♭7 8
	Ascending Melodic minor 1 2 ♭3 4 5 6 7 8
	Harmonic minor 1 2 ♭3 4 5 ♭6 7 8
	minor pentatonic 1 ♭3 4 5 ♭7 8
	Blues 1 ♭3 4 ♯4 5 ♭7 8
minor 7th (II) Function	Dorian 1 2 ♭3 4 5 6 ♭7 9
	Ascending melodic minor 1 2 ♭3 4 5 6 7 8
	Harmonic minor 1 2 ♭3 4 5 ♭6 7 1
	minor Pentatonic 1 ♭3 4 5 ♭7 8
	Blues 1 ♭3 4 ♯4 5 7 8
	diminished (start with whole step) 1 2 ♭3 4 ♯4 ♯5 6 7 8
	Seventh scale (start on the 4th) 1 2 3 4 5 6 ♭7 ♮7 8

Dominant Family

Chord Type	Scale Form
Dominant 7th unaltered 1 3 5 ♭7 9	Mixolydian 1 2 3 4 5 6 ♭7 8
	Lydian Dominant 1 2 3 ♯4 5 6 ♭7 8
	Major Pentatonic 1 2 3 5 6 8
	minor Pentatonic 1 ♭3 4 5 ♭7 8
	Blues 1 ♭3 ♮3 4 ♯4 5 ♭7 8
	Seventh scale 1 2 3 4 5 6 ♭7 ♮7 1
Dominant 7th ♯11 1 3 5 ♭7 9 ♯11	Lydian dominant 1 2 3 ♯4 5 6 ♭7 8
Dominant 7th ♭5, ♯5 or both 1 3 ♭5 ♭7 1 3 ♯5 ♭7 1 3 (♭5 ♯5) ♭7	Whole Tone 1 2 3 ♯4 ♯5 ♯6

4

Chord Type	Scale Form
Dominant 7th (♭9)	Diminished
1 3 5 ♭7 ♭9	1 ♭2 ♭3 ♮3 ♯4 5 6 ♭7 8
Dominant 7th ♯9	Diminished 1 ♭2 ♭3 ♮3 ♯4 5 ♭7 8
1 3 5 ♭7 ♯9	Diminished whole tone
	1 ♭2 ♭3 ♮3 ♯4 ♯5 ♯6 8
	Dorian 1 2 ♭3 4 5 6 ♭7 8
	Blues 1 ♭3 ♮3 4 ♯4 5 ♭7 8
	minor pentatonic 1 ♭3 4 5 ♭7 8
Dominant 7th ♭9 and ♯9	diminished 1 ♭2 ♭3 ♮3♯4 5 6 ♭7 8
	diminished whole tone
	1 ♭2 ♭3 ♮3 ♯4 ♯5 ♯6 8
	minor pentatonic 1 ♭3 4 5 ♭7 8
	Blues 1 ♭3 ♮3 4 ♯4 5 ♭7 8
Dominant 7th ♭5 and ♭9	diminished
	1 ♭2 ♭3 ♮3 ♯4 5 6 ♭7 8
	diminished whole tone
	1 ♭2 ♭3 ♮3 ♯4 ♯5 ♯6 8
	minor pentatonic 1 ♭3 4 5 ♭7 8
	Blues 1 ♭3 ♮3 4 ♯4 5 ♭7 8
Dominant 7th	diminished scale
♭5 and ♭9 13 ♭5 ♭7 ♭9	1 ♭2 ♭3 ♮3 ♯4 5 6 ♭7 8
♯5 and ♯9 13 ♯5 ♭7 ♯9	minor pentatonic
♭5 and ♯9 13 ♭5 ♭7 ♯9	1 ♭3 4 5 ♭7 8
♯5 and ♭9 13 ♯5 ♭7 ♭9	Blues 1 ♭3 ♮3 4 ♯4 5 ♭7 8
(and/combination)	

Half-diminished chords

Chord Type	Scale Form
(half-diminished 7th	Locrian 1 ♭2 ♭3 4 ♭5 ♭6 ♭7 8
(ø7)	Locrian ♯2 — 1 2 ♭3 4 ♭5 ♭6 ♭7 8
or	Seventh scale (start on ♭6)
	1 2 3 4 5 6 ♭7 ♮7 1
minor 7th (♭5)	diminished (start with whole step)
1 ♭3 ♭5 ♭7	1 2 ♭3 4 ♯4 ♯5 6 7 8
	blues 1 ♭3 4 ♯4 5 ♭7 8

diminished chords

diminished 7th	diminished scale
(o7)	(start with whole step)
1 ♭3 ♭5 6	1 2 ♭3 4 ♯4 ♯5 6 7 8

Because the scale(s) which I refer to as seventh scales have not been dealt with in any book except my Improvisational Patterns. The Bebop Era, Volumes 1, 2, and 3 (published by Charles Colin; 315 West 53rd Street; New York, N.Y. 10019), perhaps a word of explanation would be in order:

1. The scale usually moves in basic eighth note patterns.

2. The scale always starts on a downbeat and a chord tone.

3. More often than not, the scale is played in a descending fashion.

4. When playing a major scale over a I chord, an extra half step occurs between 5 and 6 if the scale starts on the root, 3rd, 5th, or 7th of the chord (1 7 6 ♭6 5 4 3 2 1).

5. When playing a mixolydian scale over a II, V7 or VII chord, an extra half step usually occurs between the tonic and the flat seventh of the scale, as in the following:

Dmi7, G7, B = G G♭ F E D C B A G
              1 7 ♭7 6 5 4 3 2 1

This rule is operative as long as the scale starts on the root, 3rd, 5th, or 7th of the V7 chord.

Owing to the importance of the seventh scale and its pervasiveness in virtually every chord playing situation, I have chosen to place the scale in brackets whenever it appears in the analyses.

Transcribing Solos From Records

One of the undersirable consequences resulting from a surfeit of teaching methods, improvisation books, and other educational aids has been the virtual disappearance of the player who accelerates learning by playing along with records.

It is lamentable that we teachers, authors, educators, and performers from the period B.J.M.B. (before jazz method books) have forgotten that we learned our craft by playing along with and studying the solos of our jazz heroes.

While no rational educator would advocate a return to those times when recordings were the principal means of learning, it behooves us to re-examine the very important role that record transcriptions can and must play in the development and continued growth of jazz players.

For the young jazz player, listening to, analyzing, and playing along with records is an absolute must if he is to learn the language, its syntax, grammar inflections, etc. The situation for the young player is not unlike that of a student learning to speak a foreign language. While books, flash cards and other visual aids are invaluable, they can never supplant hearing and imitating the spoken word. Even our native language is learned best through imitation of those around us; father, mother, brother, sister, nurse, etc. A child growing up in a French-speaking environment does not, as a consequence, speak German; he speaks French. Unless the budding jazz player is in an aural environment where the language of jazz is spoken (played), he will not learn that language. Subtlety, correct use of inflection, a feeling for swing, interpretation, style, etc., are all things that are most effectively learned through the repeated hearing of those players who first defined the music.

For the advanced jazz player, listening, analyzing, and transcribing are equally valuable if growth is to be continuous. Although the ends may be different and actual transcription, either written or played, may not take place; every good jazz player has a mandate to listen in a disciplined fashion to the music of his contemporaries. How else to stay abreast of the myriad, sometimes violent, changes taking place in this continually evolving music?

Sometimes new techniques, different approaches, new harmonic, rhythmic, and melodic ideas are more easily grasped when repeated listening is possible, hence the value, again, of record transcription.

The following aids to transcribing are offered:

1. Check turntable for key (pitch). Use common sense or some other referential, such as a tune on the album where the key is known. Adjust speed of turntable to a desired pitch.

2. Record solo on 7½ ips on tape (two levels beneath). Try to record from at least one chorus before (safety with changes, tempo, feel, etc.).

3. Listen to entire solo for:
   a. length (number of choruses)
   b. general shape, feel, form, etc.
   c. changes

4. If faster than moderate tempo, make initial transcription at half speed, 3¾ ips.
   a. If possible, transcribe one measure of phrase at a time. *Listen, sing, write.*
   b. Play preceding phrase, then new phrase as before.

If a rhythm or pitch is troublesome, try to solve it through repeated listening and isolation. If necessary, slow to 1½ ips and stop on the note or rhythm group.

If a double time persists, transcribe it as though in 4/4 time, i.e.

in finished form.

If a piece is particularly complex rhythmically, you might bar off the entire solo, transcribe the first beat in each measure, then beat 3, later filling in missing notes. Sometimes educated guesses might be made based on melodic or rhythmic practices *au courante*. A certain degree of predictability usually exists to the attuned ear.

5. Once the solo is complete, verify at half speed by playing along on your instrument. Add inflections, dynamics, accents, slurs, etc.

6. Play at the actual tempo for missed notes, etc. Verify at the actual tempo.

CLIFFORD BROWN

BIOGRAPHICAL SKETCH

1930   October 30; born in Wilmington, Delaware.

1945   Father gave him a trumpet when he entered senior high school; studied jazz harmony, theory, trumpet, piano, vibes and bass with Robert Lowery.

1948   Gigged around Philadelphia; was encouraged and influenced by Theodore "Fats" Navarro.

1949   Awarded a scholarship to Maryland State College.

1950   June; Hospitalized after an automobile accident until May 1951.

1952   March 21; made his first professional recordings in Chicago: *Ida Red, I Come From Jamaica, Blue Boy, and Darn That Dream (Ida Red* and *I Come From Jamaica* are now available on Clifford Brown: The Beginning and the End Columbia C-32284).

1952-53   Toured with the Rhythm & blues band of Chris Powell.

1953   Played with Tadd Dameron. Freelanced in New York City, recording with Tadd Dameron, Lou Donaldson, J.J. Johnson, Gigi Gryce, and Lionel Hampton in addition to his own groups. Went to California with Max Roach. From August to December also played with Lionel Hampton in a trumpet section which at that time included Quincy Jones and Art Farmer.

1954   February; recorded with the Jazz Messengers of Art Blakey live at Birdland.

Won the New Star Award in the 1954 *downbeat* Critic's Poll. Engaged in a prodigious amount of recording activity with the Clifford Brown-Max Roach Quintet and various All-Star groups in both Los Angeles and New York City.

1955   Recorded with the Brown-Roach Quintet, with the same group under the leadership of Sonny Rollins (Sonny Rollins Plus Four: Prestige LP 7038, which was also issued as Three Giants: Prestige PR 7821), and with a string orchestra.

1956   June 25; last recording at a jam session at Music City in Philadelphia (*Walkin', A Night in Tunisia,* and *Donna Lee,* all of which are on Clifford Brown: The Beginning and the End Columbia C-32284).

June 26; Clifford Brown was killed in an automobile accident on the Pennsylvania Turnpike.

Clifford Brown Genealogy Chart

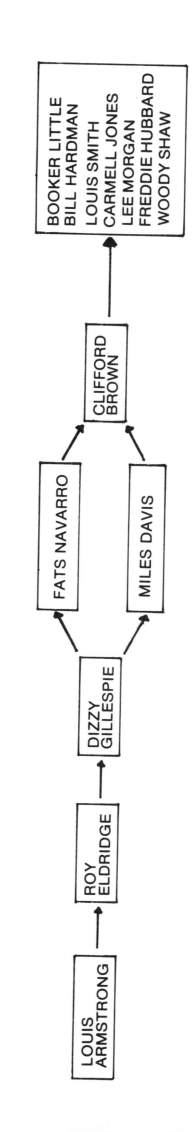

Clifford Brown: Musical Preferences

PREFERRED TUNE TYPES

1. *Standards.* Over seventy-five standards, including more than one recording on some, i.e., *All the Things You Are, What's New,* and *I Get a Kick Out of You.*

2. *Jazz Originals.* More than seventy recordings of compositions by jazz composers such as Charlie Parker, Dizzy Gillespie, J.J. Johnson, Gigi Gryce, Quincy Jones, Horace Silver, Tadd Dameron, Sonny Rollins, Harold Land, and Richie Powell.

3. *Clifford Brown Originals.* Around ten recordings of his own tunes.

4. *Blues.* Very few recordings of blues, including *The Blues Walk, Wee-Dot, Blues,* and *Now's the Time.*

5. *Contrafacts.* Few tunes based on other tunes, mainly compositions by Horace Silver, Bud Powell, et al.

6. *I Got Rhythm.* Very few, such as *Turnpike* and *Move.*

PREFERRED TEMPOS

The bulk of Brownie's recorded tempos fall between circa = 160
The bulk of Brownie's recorded tempos fall between circa = 160 and = 160. Of course, there are ballads such as *It Might as Well Be Spring* and *Ghost of a Chance* which are at very slow tempos, circa = 58 and slower. Despite his legendary and prodigious technique he used double time sparingly and judiciously.

At moderate to fast tempos his lines move basically in eighth notes with extensive use of turns and other inflections. Predictably, at ballad tempos his lines are melismatic, full of assymetrical groupings, and largely non-reiterative of the basic pulse.

PREFERRED METERS
Almost entirely 4/4 (with *Valse Hot* being a notable exception).

PREFERRED KEYS

1. B♭ and E♭ are preferred about equally.

2. F and A are preferred about equally.

3. C and D are preferred about equally.

4. Compositions also appear in D minor, F minor, C minor, E minor, a minor, G minor and E minor.

SCALE PREFERENCES

1. Major (and derivatives)

2. Seventh scale

3. Blues scale

4. Pentatonic scale

5. Chromatic scale

6. Diminished scale

RANGE
Although Clifford possessed an excellent high register, more often than not he chose to play in the bottom and middle registers with occasional and dramatic forays into the upper register. Unlike Dizzy and Fats he rarely used the extreme upper register.

MELODIC DEVICES
1. Chromaticism, which most often takes the form of upper and lower neighboring tones to various scale tones, particularly at the beginning and just before the ends of phrases.

2. Quotes. Brown, unlike most of his contemporaries, used quotes very sparingly. (Contrast his lack of use of quotes with the profuse use of quotes by one of his main influences, Fats Navarro.)

DRAMATIC DEVICES
1. Vibrato

2. Slurs, glissandi, and appogiaturas are much in evidence.

3. Varied articulation. His articulation is more varied than that of most brass players. His staccato is excellent and beautifully controlled.

4. Alternate fingerings. There is some use of alternate fingerings but much less than in the playing of Miles, Dizzy, and most contemporary trumpet players.

A Selected List of Original Tunes of Clifford Brown

Sandu

Brownie Speaks

Daahoud

Joy Spring

The Blues Walk

Minor Mood

Swingin'

George's Dilemma

Gerkin for Perkin

Selected Bibliography of Clifford Brown

Atkins, R. "Clifford Brown." *Jazz Monthly,* vol. 6 (August 1960), pp. 4-6+

Bolton, Robert. "Clifford Brown." *Jazz Journal,* vol. 22, no. 5, (May 1969), pp. 6-7.

Feather, Leonard. "Clifford Brown." *Jazz Times,* June 1980, pp. 14-15. Includes interview with Larue Brown Watson.

____. *The New Edition of the Encyclopedia of Jazz.* New York: Bonanza Books, 1962.

Gardner, Barbara. "The Legacy of Clifford Brown." *downbeat,* vol. 28, no. 21 (October 12, 1961), pp. 17-21

Gerber, A. "We Remember Clifford." *Jazz Magazine,* no. 149 (December 1967), pp. 52-57+

Green, B. "Clifford Brown: Some Reflections." *Jazz Journal,* vol. 12, no. 3 (March 1959), pp. 5-8.

Jepsen, Jorgen G. "Clifford Brown: A Complete Discography." *downbeat: Music '70* (Yearbook), pp. 109-113.

McCarthy, Albert; Morgan, Alun; Oliver, Paul; and Harrison, Max. *Jazz on Record: A Critical Guide to the First Fifty Years (1917-1967).* New York: Oak Publications, 1968.

Sheridan, Chris. "A Study in Brown." *Jazz Journal,* vol. 29, no. 6 (June 1976), pp. 4-6.

Stewart, Milton L. "Structural Development in the Jazz Improvisational Technique of Clifford Brown." Ph. D. dissertaion, University of Michigan, 1973.

West, H. "Clifford Brown: Trumpeter's Training." *downbeat,* vol. 47, no. 7 (July 1980), pp. 30-31.

Selected Discography of
Clifford Brown

Album Title	Label and No.
Clifford Brown Memorial Album	Blue Note BLP 1526/BST-81526
Brownie Eyes	Blue Note BN-LA-267-G
The Beginning and the End	Columbia C-32284
The Eminent Jay Jay Johnson, vol. 1	Blue Note BLP 1505/BST-81505
The Eminent Jay Jay Johnson, vol. 2	Blue Note BLP 1506/BST-81506
Gil Evans/Tadd Dameron: The Arrangers' Touch	Prestige PR 24049
The Complete Paris Collection	Vogue VJT-3001
Art Blakey Live at Birdland, vol. 1	Blue Note BLP-1521
Art Blakey Live at Birdland, vol. 2	Blue Note BLP-1522
The Best of Max Roach and Clifford Brown in Concert	GNP-18
Clifford Brown All-Stars	Mercury/EmArcy 36070/Trip TLP 5511
Daahoud	Mainstream 386
Remember Clifford	Mainstream 386
Three Giants	Prestige PR 7821
Study in Brown	EmArcy 36037
Clifford Brown With Max Roach: The Quintet, vol. 1	Mercury/AmArcy EMS-2-403
Jazz Immortal	World Pacific Jazz ST-20139
Art Blakey: Live Messengers	Blue Note LA 473-J2
Sonny Rollins: Saxophone Colossus and More	Prestige P-24050
Brown and Roach, Inc.	Trip TLP 5520
Clifford Brown In Paris	Prestige 24020
Jordu	EmARcy EP 1-6075/ Trip TLP 5540

ARTIST_____   Page_____

Title of composition:

Album:

Recording company:

Date:

Leader or sideman:

Instrument:

****

Tune type (circle one or more):

blues	jazz original
ballad	bebop
modal	Latin/Afro-Cuban/etc.
standard	other (specify)_____
free	

Tempo:

Key:

Dramatic devices (circle and describe):

vibrato
slurs
rips
growls
glissandi
articulation (specify):

alternate fingerings
harmonics
other (specify):

Tessitura:

Scale preferences (circle one or more):

major (and derivatives)	blues
whole tone	pentatonic
diminished	chromatic
diminished whole tone	other (specify):
lydian dominant	

_____

Prevailing scale patterns:

Recurrent patterns: (A) II V7

               Turnbacks

               Cycles

         (B) Melodic patterns

         (C) Rhythmic patterns

         (D) Other formulae (I VI II V; III VI II V; half-step progressions, etc.)

....

PERFORMANCE PRACTICE

Developmental techniques: simple to complex
(circle and describe)   complex to simple

                      single climax
                      many climaxes

                      vertical
                      horizontal

                      chord referential
                      thematic referential

                      use of sequence/call and response

                      use of quotes (what and where)

                      use of substitutions

                      rhythmic practices: double time
                                    half time
                                    assymetrical groupings
                                    reiterative
                                    non-reiterative
                      describe relationship to the basic time:

                      melody: folk-like   bluesy
                                  wide expressively   bebop
                                  narrow expressively   quartal
                                  riff-like   other (specify)_____

....

General Comments:

The musician should learn (memorize) the improvisation and play it with the record being careful to duplicate the time feel, inflections, vibrato, intensity, etc., as closely as possible. Next the player might take all of the II V7 patterns and transpose them to twelve keys varying tempo, volume, meter, register etc., until absolutely comfortable. Now the player might conceivably realize all of the II V7 situations in the tune being learned using one single pattern transposed to fit the harmonic situation. Next he should examine the various scale and melodic patterns to ascertain how the soloist uses them, then transpose the pattern to all keys, again varying musical components such as tempo, meter, volume, etc. Next he should do the same thing with cycles, turnarounds, etc., moving then from the highly specific environment of that particular composition to a more generalized musical situation.

ARTIST___Clifford Brown_____   Page_____

Title of composition: Brownie Speaks

Album: Clifford Brown Memorial Album

Recording company: Blue Note BST-81526

Date: June 9, 1953

Leader or sideman: Leader

Instrument: Trumpet

••

Tune type (circle one or more):   blues   (jazz original)
                                         ballad   (bebop)
                                         modal   Latin/Afro-Cuban/etc.
                                         standard   other (specify)_____
                                         free

Tempo: ♩ = 120

Key: Concert B♭ (trumpet key of C)

Dramatic devices (circle and describe): (vibrato)
                                         (slurs)
                                         rips
                                         growls
                                         glissandi
                                         (articulation)(specify):   varied

                                         alternate fingerings
                                         harmonics
                                         other (specify):

Tessitura: Middle

Scale preferences (circle one or more): (major)(and derivatives)   blues
                                         whole tone   pentatonic
                                         diminished   chromatic
                                         diminished whole tone   (other)(specify):
                                         lydian dominant   [ ] seventh scales

Prevailing scale patterns:

Recurrent patterns: (A) (II V7)   See attached sheet

(Turnbacks)   The entire tune consists of turnback patterns.

Cycles

(B) Melodic patterns

(C) Rhythmic patterns

(D) Other formulae (I VI II V; III VI II V; half-step progressions, etc.)

••

PERFORMANCE PRACTICE

Developmental techniques: simple to complex
(circle and describe)   complex to simple (neither)

single climax
many climaxes (neither)

(vertical)
horizontal

(chord referential)
thematic referential

use of sequence/call and response

use of quotes (what and where)

use of substitutions

rhythmic practices: double time
                     half time
                     assymetrical groupings
                     (reiterative)
                     non-reiterative
describe relationship to the basic time: straight ahead

melody: folk-like   (bluesy)
         (wide expressively)   (bebop)
         narrow expressively   quartal
         riff-like   other (specify)_____

••

General Comments:

Clifford Brown: Brownie Speaks

21

Brownie Speaks : II V₇ Patterns

Brownie Speaks : Turnarounds

The entire tune consists of turnaround patterns to be studied, i.e.,

C_7 $E\flat_7$ | $A\flat$ G_7 and C_7 $B\flat_7$ | $A\flat_7$ G_7

ARTIST___Clifford Brown_____   Page_____

Title of composition: Get Happy

Album: The Eminent Jay Jay Johnson (Blue Note BLP 1505, vol 1/Blue Note BST 81505) &
Blue Note Gems of Jazz (Blue Note BLP 82001)

Recording company: see above _____

Date: June 22, 1953

Leader or sideman: Sideman

Instrument: Trumpet

••

Tune type (circle one or more):

blues
ballad
modal
(standard)
free

jazz original
bebop
Latin/Afro-Cuban/etc.
other (specify)_____

Tempo: ♩ = 132

Key: Concert F (trumpet key of G)

Dramatic devices (circle and describe):

(vibrato)
(slurs)
rips
growls
glissandi
(articulation) (specify):   varied

alternate fingerings
harmonics
other (specify):

Tessitura: Middle

Scale preferences (circle one or more):

(major) (and derivatives)
whole tone
diminished
diminished whole tone
lydian dominant

blues
pentatonic
chromatic
(other) (specify):
[ ] seventh scales

Prevailing scale patterns:

Recurrent patterns: (A) (II V7) Each of the B sections is a splendid example of whole step descending II V7

               Turnbacks   changes and should be studied in isolation;

               Cycles   C- F7 | B♭- E♭7 | A♭- D♭7 | etc.

         (B) Melodic patterns

         (C) Rhythmic patterns

         (D) Other formulae (I VI II V; III VI II V; half-step progressions, etc.)

•••

PERFORMANCE PRACTiCE

Developmental techniques: simple to complex

(circle and describe)   complex to simple   (neither)

                  single climax

                  many climaxes   (neither)

                (vertical)

                horizontal

                (chord referential)

                thematic referential

                (use of sequence) call and response   much use of sequential patterns in the (B)

                use of quotes (what and where)   sections

                use of substitutions

                rhythmic practices: double time

                              half time

                              assymetrical groupings

                              (reiterative)

                              non-reiterative

                describe relationship to the basic time: straight ahead

                melody: folk-like   bluesy

                    (wide expressively)   (bebop)

                    narrow expressively   quartal

                    riff-like   other (specify)_____

••

General Comments:

Clifford Brown : Get Happy

ARTIST___Clifford Brown_____   Page_____

Title of composition: All the Things You Are

Album: <u>Clifford In Paris</u>

Recording company: Blue Note PR 24020 (Matrix 4660)

Date: September 29, 1953

Leader or sideman: Leader

Instrument: Trumpet

••

Tune type (circle one or more):

blues   jazz original
ballad   bebop
modal   Latin/Afro-Cuban/etc.
(standard)   other (specify)_____
free

Tempo: ♩ = 208

Key: Concert A♭ (trumpet key of B♭)

Dramatic devices (circle and describe):

(vibrato)
(slurs)
rips
growls
glissandi
(articulation)(specify): varied

alternate fingerings
harmonics
other (specify):

Tessitura: Middle

Scale preferences (circle one or more):

(major)(and derivatives)   blues
whole tone   pentatonic
diminished   chromatic
diminished whole tone   (other)(specify):
lydian dominant   <u>[   ] seventh scale</u>

Prevailing scale patterns:

Recurrent patterns: (A) (II V7)   See attached sheet

Turnbacks

Cycles

(B) Melodic patterns

(C) Rhythmic patterns

(D) Other formulae (I VI II V; III VI II V; half-step progressions, etc.)

....

PERFORMANCE PRACTICE

Developmental techniques: simple to complex
   (circle and describe)   complex to simple (neither)

single climax
(many climaxes)

(vertical)
horizontal

(chord referential)
thematic referential

(use of sequence) call and response   some use of sequence

use of quotes (what and where)

use of substitutions

rhythmic practices: (double time)
                     half time
                     assymetrical groupings
                     (reiterative)
                     non-reiterative
describe relationship to the basic time: straight ahead

melody: folk-like   bluesy
        (wide expressively)   (bebop)
        narrow expressively   quartal
        riff-like   other (specify)_____

....

General Comments:

Clifford Brown: All the Things You Are

All the Things You Are : II V7 Patterns

All the Things You Are : One-measure II V7 Patterns

ARTIST___Clifford Brown_____   Page_____

Title of composition: Confirmation

Album: A Night At Birdland

Recording company: Blue Note 1522

Date: February 21, 1954

Leader or sideman: Sideman

Instrument: Trumpet

•••

Tune type (circle one or more):   blues   (jazz original)
                                          ballad   (bebop)
                                          modal   Latin/Afro-Cuban/etc.
                                          standard   other (specify)_____
                                          free

Tempo: ♩ = 126

Key: Concert F (trumpet key of G)

Dramatic devices (circle and describe):   (vibrato)
                                                 (slurs)
                                                 rips
                                                 growls
                                                 (glissandi)
                                                 (articulation)(specify):   varied

                                                 alternate fingerings
                                                 harmonics
                                                 other (specify):

Tessitura: Low to high

Scale preferences (circle one or more):   (major)(and derivatives)   blues
                                                 whole tone   pentatonic
                                                 diminished   (chromatic)
                                                 diminished whole tone   other (specify):
                                                 lydian dominant   [   ] seventh scale
                                                                           _____

Prevailing scale patterns:

Recurrent patterns: (A) (II V7)   See attached sheet

            Turnbacks

            Cycles

       (B) Melodic patterns

       (C) Rhythmic patterns

       (D) Other formulae (I VI II V; III VI II V; half-step progressions, etc.)

....

PERFORMANCE PRACTICE

Developmental techniques: simple to complex   (neither)
(circle and describe)   complex to simple

            single climax
            (many climaxes)

            (vertical)
            horizontal

            (chord referential)
            thematic referential

            (use of sequence) call and response   some use of sequence

            use of quotes (what and where)

            use of substitutions

            rhythmic practices: double time
                           half time
                           assymetrical groupings
                           (reiterative)
                           non-reiterative
            describe relationship to the basic time: straight ahead

            melody: folk-like   bluesy
                 (wide expressively)   (bebop)
                 narrow expressively   quartal
                 riff-like   other (specify)_____

....

General Comments:

Clifford Brown: Confirmation

36

Confirmation: II V₇ Patterns

Study all of the three-measure descending II V₇ groups
which occur in measures 2 through 4 in each of the
A sections of this AABA tune.

ARTIST Clifford Brown   Page_____

Title of composition: I Don't Stand a Ghost Of a Chance With You

Album: Brown and Roach, Inc.

Recording company: EmArcy EP 1-6112 and Trip TLP 5520

Date: August 3, 1954

Leader or sideman: Co-leader

Instrument: Trumpet

•••

Tune type (circle one or more):

blues	jazz original
(ballad)	bebop
modal	Latin/Afro-Cuban/etc.
(standard)	other (specify)_____
free	

Tempo: ♩ = 58

Key: Concert C (trumpet key of D)

Dramatic devices (circle and describe):

(vibrato)
(slurs)
rips
growls
glissandi
(articulation)(specify):   very varied

alternate fingerings
harmonics
other (specify):

Tessitura: Low to middle

Scale preferences (circle one or more):

(major)(and derivatives)	(blues)
whole tone	pentatonic
(diminished)	chromatic
diminished whole tone	(other)(specify):
lydian dominant	[ ] seventh scales

Prevailing scale patterns:

Recurrent patterns: (A) II V7

                      Turnbacks

                      Cycles

          (B) Melodic patterns

          (C) Rhythmic patterns

          (D) Other formulae (I VI II V; III VI II V; half-step progressions, etc.)

•••

PERFORMANCE PRACTICE

Developmental techniques: simple to complex

(circle and describe)   complex to simple (complex throughout)

                   single climax

                   (many climaxes)

                   (vertical)

                   horizontal

                   (chord referential)

                   thematic referential

                   use of sequence/call and response

                   use of quotes (what and where)

                   (use of substitutions) particularly minor third and tritone substitutions

                   rhythmic practices: (double time)

                            half time

                           (assymetrical groupings)

                            reiterative

                         (non-reiterative)

                   describe relationship to the basic time: floating

                   melody: folk-like   bluesy

                           (wide expressively)   (bebop)

                           narrow expressively   quartal

                           riff-like   other (specify)_____

•••

General Comments:

Clifford Brown : I Don't Stand a Ghost Of a Chance With You

42

ARTIST___Clifford Brown_____   Page_____

Title of composition: Joy Spring

Album: Jordu

Recording company: EmArcy EP 1-6075 and Trip TLP 5540

Date: August 6, 1954

Leader or sideman: Co-leader

Instrument: Trumpet

****

Tune type (circle one or more):   blues   (jazz original)
                                          ballad   (bebop)
                                          modal   Latin/Afro-Cuban/etc.
                                          standard   other (specify)_____
                                          free

Tempo: ♩ = 160

Key: Concert F (trumpet key of G)

Dramatic devices (circle and describe):   (vibrato)
                                           (slurs)
                                           rips
                                           growls
                                           glissandi
                                           (articulation)(specify):   varied

                                           alternate fingerings
                                           harmonics
                                           other (specify):

Tessitura: Middle

Scale preferences (circle one or more):   (major)(and derivatives)   (blues)
                                           whole tone   pentatonic
                                           diminished   chromatic
                                           diminished whole tone   (other)(specify):
                                           lydian dominant   [ ] seventh scale

Prevailing scale patterns:

Recurrent patterns: (A) (II V7)   The entire tune is an excellent study in one measure II V7 patterns,
often in double time figures.

       Turnbacks

       Cycles

   (B) Melodic patterns

   (C) Rhythmic patterns

   (D) Other formulae (I VI II V; III VI II V; half-step progressions, etc.)

••

PERFORMANCE PRACTICE

Developmental techniques: simple to complex   (neither)
   (circle and describe)   complex to simple

       single climax
       (many climaxes)

       (vertical)
       horizontal

       (chord referential)
       thematic referential

       (use of sequence) call and response   much use of sequence in the bridge

       (use of quotes) (what and where)   hints at "Mexican Hat Dance" in the first
bridge

       use of substitutions

       rhythmic practices: (double time)
               half time
               assymetrical groupings
               reiterative
               non-reiterative
   describe relationship to the basic time: straight ahead

     melody: folk-like   (bluesy)
          (wide expressively)   (bebop)
          narrow expressively   quartal
          riff-like   other (specify)————

••

General Comments:

Clifford Brown : Joy Spring

ARTIST___Clifford Brown_____   Page_____

Title of composition: The Blues Walk

Album: Jordu

Recording company: EmArcy MG 36036 and Trip TLP-5540

Date: February 23, 1955

Leader or sideman: Co-leader

Instrument: Trumpet

****

Tune type (circle one or more):

(blues)   (jazz original)
ballad   (bebop)
modal   Latin/Afro-Cuban/etc.
standard   other (specify)_____
free

Tempo: ♩ = 132

Key: Concert B♭ (trumpet key of C)

Dramatic devices (circle and describe):

(vibrato)
(slurs)
 rips
 growls
(glissandi)
(articulation) (specify): varied

(alternate fingerings)
 harmonics
 other (specify):

Tessitura: Low to high

Scale preferences (circle one or more):

(major) (and derivatives)   (blues)
whole tone   (pentatonic)
diminished   chromatic
diminished whole tone   (other) (specify):
lydian dominant   [   ] seventh scale

Prevailing scale patterns:

Recurrent patterns: (A) (II V7) See attached sheet

                Turnbacks

                Cycles

      (B) Melodic patterns

      (C) Rhythmic patterns

      (D) Other formulae (I VI II V; III VI II V; half-step progressions, etc.)

• •

PERFORMANCE PRACTICE

Developmental techniques: (simple to complex)
    (circle and describe)   complex to simple

                    (single climax)
                    many climaxes

                    (vertical)
                    horizontal

                    (chord referential)
                    thematic referential

                    use of sequence/call and response

                    use of quotes (what and where)

                    use of substitutions

                    rhythmic practices: double time
                                      half time
                                      assymetrical groupings
                                    (reiterative)
                                    non-reiterative
                    describe relationship to the basic time: straight ahead

                    melody: folk-like   bluesy
                          (wide expressively)   (bebop)
                          narrow expressively   quartal
                        riff-like   other (specify)_____

• •

General Comments:

Clifford Brown : The Blues Walk

The Blues Walk: II V₇ Patterns

ARTIST___Clifford Brown_____   Page_____

Title of composition: What Is This Thing Called Love

Album: Clifford Brown and Max Roach At Basin Street

Recording company: EmArcy 36070 and Trip TLP 5511

Date: January 4, 1956

Leader or sideman: Co-leader

Instrument: Trumpet

••

Tune type (circle one or more):

blues
ballad
modal
(standard)
free

jazz original
bebop
Latin/Afro-Cuban/etc.
other (specify)_____

Tempo: ♩= 152

Key: Concert C (trumpet key of D)

Dramatic devices (circle and describe):

(vibrato)
(slurs)
rips
growls
glissandi
(articulation)(specify):   varied

alternate fingerings
harmonics
other (specify):

Tessitura: low to high

Scale preferences (circle one or more):

(major)(and derivatives)
whole tone
diminished
diminished whole tone
lydian dominant

blues
pentatonic
chromatic
(other)(specify):
[   ]seventh scale

Prevailing scale patterns:

Recurrent patterns: (A) (II V7)   See attached   sheet

             Turnbacks

             Cycles

     (B) Melodic patterns

     (C) Rhythmic patterns

     (D) Other formulae (I VI II V; III VI II V; half-step progressions, etc.)

....

PERFORMANCE PRACTICE

Developmental techniques: simple to complex
   (circle and describe)   complex to simple (neither)

             single climax
             (many climaxes)

             (vertical)
             horizontal

             (chord referential)
             thematic referential

             use of sequence/call and response

             use of quotes (what and where)

             use of substitutions

             rhythmic practices: double time
                             half time
                             assymetrical groupings
                             (reiterative)
                             non-reiterative
           describe relationship to the basic time: straight ahead

melody: folk-like   bluesy
        (wide expressively)   (bebop)
        narrow expressively   quartal
        riff-like   other (specify)_____

....

General Comments:

Clifford Brown: What Is This Thing Called Love

55

What Is This Thing Called Love: II V₇ Patterns

ARTIST___Clifford Brown_____   Page_____

Title of composition: I'll Remember April

Album: Clifford Brown and Max Roach At Basin Street

Recording company: EmArcy 36070 and Trip TLP 5511

Date: January 4, 1956

Leader or sideman: Co-leader

Instrument: Trumpet

••

Tune type (circle one or more):

blues	jazz original
ballad	bebop
modal	Latin/Afro-Cuban/etc.
(standard)	other (specify)_____
free	

Tempo: $\quad \downarrow$ = 160

Key: Concert G (trumpet key of A)

Dramatic devices (circle and describe):

(vibrato)
(slurs)
rips
growls
glissandi
(articulation)(specify):   varied

alternate fingerings
harmonics
other (specify):

Tessitura: Low to middle

Scale preferences (circle one or more):

(major)(and derivatives)	blues
whole tone	pentatonic
diminished	(chromatic)
diminished whole tone	(other)(specify):
(lydian dominant)	seventh scale

Prevailing scale patterns:

Recurrent patterns: (A) (II V7)   See attached sheet

                       Turnbacks

                       Cycles

            (B) Melodic patterns

            (C) (Rhythmic patterns) 3 against 4

            (D) Other formulae (I VI II V; III VI II V; half-step progressions, etc.)

• •

PERFORMANCE PRACTICE

Developmental techniques: simple to complex
   (circle and describe)   complex to simple   (neither)

                  single climax
                  (many climaxes)

                  (vertical)
                  horizontal

                  (chord referential)
                  thematic referential

                  (use of sequence) call and response

                  (use of quotes) (what and where)   "Minute Waltz" (G) 1-3

                  use of substitutions

                  rhythmic practices: double time
                                  half time
                                  assymetrical groupings
                                (reiterative)
                                non-reiterative
                  describe relationship to the basic time: straight ahead

                  melody: folk-like   bluesy
                       (wide expressively)   (bebop)
                      narrow expressively   quartal
                      riff-like   other (specify)_____

• •

General Comments:

Clifford Brown : I'll Remember April

62

I'll Remember April: II V₇ Patterns

ARTIST_____Clifford Brown_____   Page_____

Title of composition: Gertrude's Bounce

Album: Clifford Brown and Max Roach At Basin Street

Recording company: EmArcy 36070 and Tripp TLP 5511

Date: January 4, 1956

Leader or sideman: Co-leader

Instrument: Trumpet

••

Tune type (circle one or more):   blues   (jazz original)
                                       ballad   (bebop)
                                       modal   Latin/Afro-Cuban/etc.
                                       standard   other (specify)_____
                                       free

Tempo: ♩ = 126

Key: Concert B♭ (trumpet key of C)

Dramatic devices (circle and describe):   (vibrato)
                                            (slurs)
                                            rips
                                            growls
                                            glissandi
                                            (articulation)(specify): varied

                                            alternate fingerings
                                            harmonics
                                            other (specify):

Tessitura: Middle to high

Scale preferences (circle one or more):   (major)(and derivatives)   blues
                                           whole tone   pentatonic
                                           (diminished)   (chromatic)
                                           diminished whole tone   other (specify):
                                           lydian dominant   _____

Prevailing scale patterns:

Recurrent patterns: (A) II V7   See attached sheet.

          Turnbacks

          Cycles

   (B) Melodic patterns

   (C) Rhythmic patterns

   (D) Other formulae (I VI II V; III VI II V; half-step progressions, etc.)
         The entire solo is an excellent study in the I VI II V progression.

• •

PERFORMANCE PRACTICE

Developmental techniques: simple to complex   (neither)
  (circle and describe)   complex to simple

       single climax
       (many climaxes)

       (vertical)
       horizontal

       (chord referential)
       thematic referential

       use of sequence/call and response

       use of quotes (what and where)

       use of substitutions

       rhythmic practices: double time
                    half time
                    assymetrical groupings
                    (reiterative)
                    non-reiterative
       describe relationship to the basic time: straight ahead

       melody: folk-like   bluesy
            (wide expressively)   (bebop)
            narrow expressively   quartal
            riff-like   other (specify)_____

• •

General Comments:

Clifford Brown : Gertrude's Bounce

Gertrude's Bounce: Modified II V₇ Patterns

ARTIST Clifford Brown   Page_____

Title of composition: Pent -Up House

Album: Sonny Rollins Plus Four (Prestige LP 7038) & Three Giants (Prestige PR 7821) Matrix 867

Recording company: See above

Date: March 22, 1956

Leader or sideman: Sideman

Instrument: Trumpet

****

Tune type (circle one or more):

blues   (jazz original)
ballad   (bebop)
modal   Latin/Afro-Cuban/etc.
standard   other (specify)_____
free

Tempo: ♩ = 96

Key: Concert G (trumpet Key of A)

Dramatic devices (circle and describe):

(vibrato)
(slurs)
rips
growls
glissandi
(articulation) (specify):

alternate fingerings
harmonics
other (specify):

Tessitura: Middle

Scale preferences (circle one or more):

(major) (and derivatives)   blues
whole tone   pentatonic
diminished   (chromatic)
diminished whole tone   (other) (specify):
lydian dominant   _____[ ]seventh scale_____

Prevailing scale patterns:

Recurrent patterns: (A) (II V7)   See attached sheet

                    Turnbacks

                    Cycles

        (B) Melodic patterns

        (C) Rhythmic patterns

        (D) Other formulae (I VI II V; III VI II V; half-step progressions, etc.)

• •

PERFORMANCE PRACTICE

Developmental techniques: simple to complex (neither)
(circle and describe)   complex to simple

                    single climax
                    (many climaxes)

                    (vertical)
                    horizontal

                    (chord referential)
                    thematic referential

                    (use of sequence) call and response   much   use of sequence

                    use of quotes (what and where)

                    use of substitutions

                    rhythmic practices: double time
                                   half time
                                   assymetrical groupings
                                   (reiterative)
                                 non-reiterative
                  describe relationship to the basic time: straight ahead

                  melody: folk-like   bluesy
                         (wide expressively)   (bebop)
                         narrow expressively   quartal
                         riff-like   other (specify)_____

• •

General Comments: Excellent study in II V7 I patterns.

Clifford Brown: Pent-Up House

Pent-Up House: II V₇ Patterns

76

ARTIST <u>Clifford Brown</u>   Page_____

Title of composition: Valse Hot

Album: <u>Sonny Rollins Plus Four</u> (Prestibe LP 7038) & Three Giants (Prestige PR 7821) Matrix 869

Recording company: See above

Date: March 22, 1956

Leader or sideman: Sideman

Instrument: Trumpet

****

Tune type (circle one or more):

blues	(jazz original)
ballad	(bebop)
modal	Latin/Afro-Cuban/etc.
standard	other (specify)_____
free	

Tempo: ♩ = 116

Key: Concert A♭(trumpet key of B♭)

Dramatic devices (circle and describe):

(vibrato)
(slurs)
rips
growls
glissandi
(articulation)(specify): varied

alternate fingerings
harmonics
other (specify):

Tessitura: Low to Middle

Scale preferences (circle one or more):

(major)(and derivatives)	blues
whole tone	pentatonic
diminished	(chromatic)
diminished whole tone	(other)(specify):
lydian dominant	___ ♭seventh scale ___

Prevailing scale patterns:

Recurrent patterns: (A) (II V7) See attached sheet

        Turnbacks

        Cycles

    (B) Melodic patterns

    (C) Rhythmic patterns

    (D) Other formulae (I VI II V; III VI II V; half-step progressions, etc.)

· ·

PERFORMANCE PRACTICE

Developmental techniques: (simple to complex to simple)
    (circle and describe)   complex to simple

        (single climax)
        many climaxes

        (vertical)
        horizontal

        (chord referential)
        thematic referential

        use of sequence/call and response

        use of quotes (what and where)

        use of substitutions

        rhythmic practices: (double time)
                      half time
                      assymetrical groupings
                      reiterative
                      non-reiterative
        describe relationship to the basic time: straight ahead

        melody: folk-like   bluesy
             (wide expressively)   (bebop)
             narrow expressively   quartal
             riff-like   other (specify)⎯⎯⎯⎯

· ·

General Comments:

Clifford Brown: Valse Hot

Valse Hot : II V₇ Patterns

ARTIST___Clifford Brown_____   Page_____

Title of composition: Kiss and Run

Album: <u>Sonny Rollins Plus Four</u> (Prestige LP 7038) & <u>Three Giants</u> (Prestige PR 7821) Matrix 867

Recording company: See above

Date: March 22, 1956

Leader or sideman: Sideman

Instrument: Trumpet

••

Tune type (circle one or more):

blues   (jazz original)
ballad   (bebop)
modal   Latin/Afro-Cuban/etc.
standard   other (specify)_____
free

Tempo: ♩ = 126

Key: Concert B♭ (trumpet key of C)

Dramatic devices (circle and describe):

(vibrato)
(slurs)
rips
growls
(glissandi)
(articulation)(specify):   varied

alternate fingerings
harmonics
other (specify):

Tessitura: Middle

Scale preferences (circle one or more):

(major)(and derivatives)   blues
whole tone   pentatonic
diminished   chromatic
diminished whole tone   (other)(specify):
lydian dominant   ___|seventh scale_____

Prevailing scale patterns:

Recurrent patterns: (A) (II V7)   See attached sheet

                      Turnbacks

                 (Cycles)   See attached sheet

          (B) Melodic patterns

          (C) Rhythmic patterns

          (D) Other formulae (I VI II V; III VI II V; half-step progressions, etc.)

••

PERFORMANCE PRACTICE

Developmental techniques: simple to complex
   (circle and describe)   complex to simple (neither)

                    single climax
                    (many climaxes)

                    (vertical)
                    horizontal

                    (chord referential)
                    thematic referential

                    (use of sequence) call and response   much use of sequence

                    use of quotes (what and where)

                    use of substitutions

                    rhythmic practices: double time
                                    half time
                                    assymetrical groupings
                                  (reiterative)
                                  non-reiterative
                  describe relationship to the basic time: straight ahead

                  melody: folk-like   bluesy
                         (wide expressively)   (bebop)
                         narrow expressively   quartal
                         riff-like   other (specify)_____

••

General Comments:

Clifford Brown : Kiss and Run

85

Kiss and Run : II V₇ Patterns

Kiss and Run: Whole Step Descending II V7 Patterns

Kiss and Run : Cycles

ARTIST Clifford Brown   Page_____

Title of composition: Walkin'

Album: Clifford Brown: The Beginning and the End

Recording company: Coumbia C-32284

Date: June 25,1956

Leader or sideman: Sideman

Instrument: Trumpet

•••

Tune type (circle one or more):

(blues)   jazz original
ballad   (bebop)
modal   Latin/Afro-Cuban/etc.
standard   other (specify)_____
free

Tempo: ♩ = 208

Key: Concert F (trumpet key of G)

Dramatic devices (circle and describe):

(vibrato)
(slurs)
rips
growls
glissandi
(articulation)(specify): varied

alternate fingerings
harmonics
other (specify):

Tessitura: Middle to high

Scale preferences (circle one or more):

(major)(and derivatives)   (blues)
whole tone   pentatonic
diminished   (chromatic)
diminished whole tone   (other)(specify):
lydian dominant   seventh scale

Prevailing scale patterns:

Recurrent patterns: (A) (II V7)

                Turnbacks

                Cycles

        (B) Melodic patterns

        (C) Rhythmic patterns

        (D) Other formulae (I VI II V; III VI II V; half-step progressions, etc.)

· ·

PERFORMANCE PRACTICE

Developmental techniques: simple to complex   Neither
    (circle and describe)   complex to simple

                single climax
                (many climaxes)

                (vertical)
                horizontal

                (chord referential)
                thematic referential

                use of sequence/call and response

                use of quotes (what and where)

                use of substitutions

                rhythmic practices: (double time)
                                  half time
                                  (assymetrical groupings)
                                (reiterative)
                                non-reiterative
              describe relationship to the basic time:

                      Straight Ahead

              melody: folk-like   (bluesy)
                      (wide expressively)   (bebop)
                      narrow expressively   quartal
                      riff-like   other (specify)_____

· ·

General Comments:

Clifford Brown : Walkin'

94

Walkin': II V₇ Patterns

ARTIST_____Clifford Brown_____   Page_____

Title of composition: Donna Lee

Album: Clifford Brown: The Beginning And The End

Recording company: COLUMBIA C-32284

Date: June 25, 1956

Leader or sideman: Sideman

Instrument: Trumpet

••

Tune type (circle one or more):

blues	(jazz original)
ballad	(bebop)
modal	Latin/Afro-Cuban/etc.
standard	(other) (specify)_____
free	Back Home Again In Indiana

Tempo: ♩ = 144

Key: Concert A♭ (Trumpet Key of B♭)

Dramatic devices (circle and describe):

(vibrato)
(slurs)
rips
growls
glissandi
(articulation) (specify): Varied

alternate fingerings
harmonics
other (specify):

Tessitura: Low to High

Scale preferences (circle one or more):

(major (and derivatives))	(blues)
whole tone	pentatonic
diminished	(chromatic)
diminished whole tone	(other) (specify):
lydian dominant	
	_____
	Seventh Scale

Prevailing scale patterns:

Recurrent patterns: (A) (II V7)   See attached sheet

Turnbacks

Cycles

(B) Melodic patterns

(C) Rhythmic patterns

(D) Other formulae (I VI II V; III VI II V; half-step progressions, etc.)

....

PERFORMANCE PRACTICE

Developmental techniques: simple to complex
(circle and describe)   complex to simple (neither)

single climax
(many climaxes)

(vertical)
horizontal

(chord referential)
thematic referential

use of sequence/call and response

use of quotes (what and where)

use of substitutions

rhythmic practices: double time
                    half time
                    assymetrical groupings
                    (reiterative)
                    non-reiterative
describe relationship to the basic time: straight time

melody: folk-like   bluesy
        (wide expressively)   (bebop)
        narrow expressively   quartal
        riff-like   other (specify)_____

....

General Comments:

Clifford Brown : Donna Lee

Donna Lee : II V₇ Patterns

The Language

All of the II V7 and melodic patterns, cycles, turnarounds, etc., which have been abstracted from a wide variety of musical situations, have been transposed to the key of C. In order to derive maximum benefits from their study, the reader is encouraged to transpose the patterns to all keys, varying musical components such as tempo, meter, volume, register, vibrato and articulation.

Whenever possible, the author has grouped many of the melodic patterns according to scale or mode; e.g., lydian dominant patterns, diminished patterns, etc. This practice allows the student to see at a glance the soloist's scale preferences in a variety of musical environs. (The chord to scale syllabus in the front of this book will be an invaluable aid in determining why and how the soloist chose a particular scale).

Once the material has been understood and internalized, the reader should begin striving to personalize the myriad patterns and scales in a way compatible with his/her own musical philosophy.

Finally, this series of style studies provides the jazz musician/teacher at whatever level of development the unique opportunity to "study with" John Coltrane, Miles Davis, Charlie Parker, et al.

Clifford Brown: Selected II V₇ Patterns

108

Clifford Brown: III VI II V₇ Patterns

Clifford Brown: Turnarounds

Clifford Brown : Melodic Patterns

JAZZ IMPROVISATION BOOKS
from CPP/Belwin

COMPLETE METHOD FOR IMPROVISATION
For All Instruments
____ (SB84)

This uniquely organized method by Jerry Coker devotes a thorough chapter to each of the prevailing tune-types of jazz — standard, be-bop, modal, blues, contemporary, ballad and free form — listing and discussing their characteristics and illustrating approaches to understanding and performing each type of tune. Includes one cassette.

DRONES FOR IMPROVISATION
____ (SB253)

Coltrane understood the power of playing over a properly prepared drone. Jerry Coker makes drones understandable and usable. Coker has prepared the text to help musicians utilize this little-known device in creating exciting improvisations. Tom Norris has prepared the 60-minute cassette. Here's a chance to finally explore the mystery of drones!

JAZZ KEYBOARD
For Pianists and Non-Pianists
____ (SB248)

This book is by a man who has set the standard for jazz and improvisation learning materials — Jerry Coker. A compilation of 15 years of experience in teaching jazz keyboard in several universities, this is a landmark volume. Also containing a teacher's supplement, JAZZ KEYBOARD is usable for classroom or individual study. If you are a pianist or other instrumentalist, arranger, composer, accompanist, director or teacher, you need this book!

HOW TO CREATE JAZZ CHORD PROGRESSIONS
____ (SB61)

Chuck Marohnic gives the keyboard player a basic vocabulary of scales and chords, chord changes and voicings that will help the confusion of jazz improvising disappear. Included is information concerning the cycle of fifths, the III-V-I progression, chord substitutions, cycle extensions, blues, turn-arounds, relative majors and minors and more.

PENTATONIC SCALES FOR JAZZ IMPROVISATION
____ (SB9)

More than a pattern book, this 80-page spiral-bound book by Ramon Ricker lays out the theory behind the use of pentatonic scales in jazz, then follows that up with 12 pages of transcribed solos and 40 pages of exercises to help the improviser master his new-found knowledge. Still a favorite after 11 years, this book has become a standard in the field.

TECHNIQUE DEVELOPMENT IN FOURTHS FOR JAZZ IMPROVISATION
____ (SB17)

This book in the Ramon Ricker Jazz Improvisation Series is for the advanced player. The interval of a fourth is an integral part of jazz improvisation and the sixty pages of reading and exercises will give the musician a good understanding of the interval's uses. The serious student should use this book as a supplement to aid and expand his harmonic and melodic vocabulary. When fourths are mastered, they can be applied directly to jazz improvisation and ultimately increase musicianship.

Genius Of Jazz Series Piano

Advanced and intermediate solos in the artists' own arrangements. Beautiful editions with sketch biographies.

The Genius of...
DUKE ELLINGTON
Volume 1 (TPF0024)
Two dozen tunes - the Duke's own style. Includes: I'm Nobody's Baby / I'll See You In My Dreams / I Cried For You / At Sundown / You Are My Lucky Star.

Volume 2 (TPF0157)
17 more of Ellington's best including: Black Beauty / It Don't Mean A Thing (If It Ain't Got That Swing) / Mood Indigo / Satin Doll / Sophisticated Lady.

The Genius of...
DAVE BRUBECK
Book 1 (TPF0130)
Contents: Bluette / Bossa Nova U.S.A. / Castillian Blues / Countdown / In Your Own Sweet Way / Three To Get Ready / Weep No More / Summer Song and 6 more plus Paul Desmond's "Take Five". Piano solos.

Book 2 (TPF0131)
Contents: Blue Rondo A La Turk / Kathy's Waltz / It's A Raggy Waltz / Three's A Crowd / The Duke / My One Bad Habit and 6 more piano solos.

The Genius Continues... (TPF0137)
Features 18 new previously unpublished pieces from the most recent recordings of the Dave Brubeck Quartet. The pieces have been carefully arranged and edited to ensure playability at the intermediate level. Contents include: I'd Walk A Country Mile / Mr. Fats / The Summer Music / Tritonis / We All Remember Paul and a dozen more.

The Genius of...
BENNY GOLSON (TPF0139)
Partial contents: I Remember Clifford / Out Of The Past / Along Came Betty / Blues March.

The Genius of...
GEORGE SHEARING
Volume One (TPF0052B)
Partial contents: Blue Moon / Killing Me Softly With His Song / Try A Little Tenderness / Little Things Mean A Lot.

Volume Four (TPF0055)
Partial contents: So Rare / Charmaine / April Love / Time On My Hands / How About You / At Sundown.

Volume Five (TPF0136)
Eighteen memorable tunes in the inimitable Shearing style. Including : A Certain Smile / I Cried For You / Love Is Just Around The Corner / If I Had You / It's Easy To Remember.

The Genius of...
ART TATUM (TPF0077)
32 piano solos arranged by Art Tatum. Contents includes: Goodnight Sweetheart / I'm Coming Virginia / Wabash Blues / At Sundown / If I Had You / I'm In The Mood For Love / Stompin' At The Savoy / When I Grow Too Old To Dream / Blue Moon / Sunday and more!

The Genius of...
THOMAS "FATS" WALLER (TPF0120)
Personality — jazz — piano solos. The artist's own arrangements of titles he made famous. Pianists will find no better "Fat's" selection. Twenty titles include: All That Meat And No Potatoes / Margie / I'm Sitting On Top Of The World / Who's Sorry Now / I'm Nobody's Baby and a special bonus section of selected songs from the Broadway musical "Ain't Misbehavin'."

The Genius of...
TEDDY WILSON (TPF0075)
Partial contents: Stumbling / Rose Room / Tiger Rag / I'm Thru With Love / Once In A While / Temptation.